Resolutions
of a
SAINTLY
Scholar

Resolutions
of a
SAINTLY
Scholar

Jonathan Edwards

Introduction by
Robert E. Coleman

World Wide Publications

Resolutions of a Saintly Scholar
© 1974 by Robert E. Coleman
Used by permission

Published by World Wide Publications 1992
in cooperation with the
Billy Graham Institute of Evangelism

ISBN: 0-89066-229-0
Printed in the United States of America

Contents

Introduction

Chapter 1
His Spiritual Delight
15

Chapter 2
Personal Resolutions
23

Chapter 3
Constant Review
35

Introduction

Among the shapers of American intellectual and religious history, no man stands out more brilliantly than Jonathan Edwards. His vigorous thought and exemplary life gave leadership to the Great Awakening of the eighteenth century, and laid the foundation for a new rationale of transforming personal experience of far-reaching consequence. Though the Puritan cause he espoused largely has been rejected, the voice of Edwards still can be heard through the pretense of human sufficiency, reminding us that only God is great, and that finally before Him every knee shall bow. Hurried students today, especially those engaged in theological pursuits, could well afford to spend some time with this saintly sage—one of the world's most renowned Christian scholars.

He was born at East Windsor, Connecticut, October 5, 1703, the fifth child and only son of Reverend and Mrs. Timothy Edwards' eleven children. His unusual mental and spiritual aptitude began appearing very early. He was studying Latin under his father by the time he was six. When he was ten he composed a tract on the immaterial nature of the soul. At eleven, he was writing scientific observations on insects, followed by an essay on the rainbow. Soon he was contemplating the philosophic significance of atomic physics, and grappling with such weighty problems as the meaning of personal identity, mind-body relationship, causation, and the limits of knowledge.

Just before his thirteenth birthday, the fledgling genius entered Yale College. He graduated at the head of his class of ten members in 1720; then continued studies in theology for two more years, preparing for ordination to the ministry. Licensed to preach in 1722, he went to New York City and pastored a small Presbyterian church. His work was well received, but after eight months he returned home to give himself more fully to serious study. The following year he received the Master of Arts from Yale, and was elected as a tutor.

In 1726 he accepted a call as pastoral assistant to his aging maternal grandfather, the Reverend Solomon Stoddard, at Northampton, Massachusetts. Three years later, Stoddard died, and his grandson assumed full responsibility for the large, wealthy congregation, at the time the most influential parish in New England.

Shortly after beginning his new office Edwards married Sarah Pierpont of New Haven. She was a lady of rare piety and prudence. Her ability to assume most of the domestic cares of the house enabled her husband to pursue his work without undue interruptions. They shared a common sense of mission. During their beautiful married life of thirty years, they prayed together at least once a day, unless something extraordinary happened.

Into their home eleven children were born. Early the ten girls and one son were taught the meaning of reverence. Family prayers always preceded the business of the day, and after supper each evening, Edwards took an hour with his family to converse on the things of God. Probably the highest tribute that can be paid to Jonathan and Sarah Edwards is that all their children followed in the way of their godly parents.

The loving father and pastor lived an exacting example of personal discipline. Every waking moment was regimented to his holy calling. Periods were established for eating, physical exercise, and sleep, but only as they were necessary to assure alertness of mind. It was not uncommon for him to spend thirteen hours a day in his study, beginning at four o'clock in the morning. When making calls by horseback, he continued his meditations and would jot fleeting ideas down on paper. Though never strong in body, he constantly practiced self-denial. On occasion, he set aside whole days for fasting and self-examination. With a consuming thirst for knowledge, he read all the books he could obtain on a wide range of subjects. Supremely, though, he fixed his attention upon the Bible, the sole authority for his faith and ministry.

Out of this consecrated devotion he prepared his masterful sermons. Seldom have more profound messages been delivered. His words were precise, set in simple speech and fell with such solemn weight upon the hearers that few could turn away unmoved. Even more significant were the literary works which flowed from his pen. His published writings eventually developed into a small theological library.

In 1731 he was first brought into national prominence by the publication of a formal theological lecture entitled *God Glorified in Man's Dependence*. This reasoned discourse established the quiet scholar as a worthy defender of Calvinism against the challenge of a decadent Arminianism rising in his day. Edwards' message was unequivocal. God is sovereign. He owes man nothing, nor can man add anything to God's perfection by good works. Divine grace alone offers any hope or meaning to human existence. All man can do is receive God's love through Jesus Christ.

Nourished by such teaching, Northampton experienced a gracious revival in 1734 and 1735. It extended to every part of town, and someone in nearly every household was touched. More than 300 persons were converted within a few months. The whole character of the community was changed. Responding to many inquiries, an account of the work of grace was published by Edwards under the title *A Faithful Narrative of the Surprising Work of God in the Conversion of Many Hundred Souls* (1736).

Again, in 1740, his parish was the scene of mighty spiritual renewal. George Whitefield, the famous evangelist, visited Northampton at its height and became a close friend of Edwards. Fanned by the preaching of these and other men, revival fires spread throughout New England. Hundreds of cold churches and thousands of people were quickened by the Spirit of God. The famous Enfield sermon, *Sinners in the Hands of an Angry God,* belongs to this period.

But as is true of all movements among men, there were some abuses which caused controversy. To counteract some of the misunderstandings, Edwards wrote *Distinguishing Marks of a Work of God* (1741), showing the difference between genuine and false experience. Another defense of the revival against the objections of its opponents was *Thoughts Concerning the Present Revival of Religion in New England* (1742). *A Treatise Concerning Religious Affections* (1746) also came out of this era, his classic treatment of subjective spiritual experience, in which he concludes: "The essence of all true religion lies in holy love."

Tension in the church began to surface when Edwards reprimanded some young people from prominent families for reading unclean books. It reached a climax when the pastor reversed a policy of his predecessor by insisting that only persons professing a living faith in Jesus Christ be admitted to Holy Communion. Finally, the matter went before a church council, which in 1750 requested that Edwards leave. Such is the fickleness of human nature. Sometimes people that have known the greatest privilege have become the most ungrateful.

The faithful pastor received his rejection with resignation to the will of God. There was no bitterness or rancor toward his antagonists. His *Farewell Sermon* is one of the purest examples of a loving shepherd's concern ever written.

Of the places of service offered to him, Edwards accepted a call to Stockbridge, a mission post on the frontier. There he assumed the care of a small congregation, while ministering to the Housatonic and Mohawk Indians of the area. Demands of the wilderness life, learning a new language, and frequent sickness were no deterrent to his faith. However, all was not peaceful. Quarrels among the settlers and shameless exploitation of the Indians by unscrupulous whites made his work difficult. Yet he patiently held up the Word of Life, and sought to lead his people in a more excellent way.

In this remote setting he was able to bring to completion many of his major works. His greatest, *Freedom of the Will,* was finished in 1754. Endeavoring to make the eternal decrees of God accord more with the prevailing notions of human freedom, he emphasized that man has the natural power to serve God if he chooses; but he will not be so inclined unless God reveals Himself as man's highest good. Still the choice belongs to man. The idea was further clarified in *Original Sin Defended* (1758). Other notable works of this period, published posthumously, were *The Nature of True Virtue* (1765), *The End for Which God Created the World* (1765), and the monumental *History of the Work of Redemption* (1774).

In 1757 Edwards was elected to the presidency of the College of New Jersey. It seemed at last that he would be in an environment congenial to his academic talents. But soon after arriving at Princeton, before he could be joined by his wife, complications developed from smallpox inoculation, and he died on March 22, 1758. He was fifty-four years of age.

When he knew that the end was near, he said to his daughter with him:

> Dear Lucy, it seems to me to be the will of God that I must shortly leave you; therefore give my kindest love to my dear wife. Tell her that the uncommon union which has so long subsisted between us, has been of such a nature as, I trust, is spiritual, and therefore will continue forever; and I hope she will be supported under so great a trial, and submit cheerfully to the will of God. And as to my children, you are now like to be left fatherless; which I hope will be an inducement to you all to seek a Father who will never fail you.

The last he was heard to say, addressing some friends at his bedside, was: "Trust in God, and you need not fear."

These words reflect the spirit by which Jonathan Edwards lived. He was a man "swallowed up" in his Father's will. Whatever happened, he knew that God never made a mistake.

1

His Spiritual Delight

This explicit trust in the providence of God seems to have come into focus toward the latter part of his college course. Reflecting upon it years later, he recounts in his own *Personal Narrative* how "not only a conviction, but a delightful conviction" of God's absolute sovereignty broke upon his consciousness.

The first that I remember that ever I found anything of that sort of inward, sweet delight in God and divine things, that I have lived much in since, was on reading those words: *"Now unto the King eternal, immortal, invisible, the only wise God, be honour and glory for ever and ever. Amen"* (1 Timothy 1:17). As I read the words, there came into my soul, and was as it were diffused through it, a sense of the glory of the divine Being; a new sense, quite different from anything I ever experienced before. Never any words of Scripture seemed to me as these words did. I thought with myself, how excellent a being that was; and how happy I should be, if I might enjoy that God, and be wrapt up to God in heaven, and be as it were swallowed up in Him. I kept saying, and as it were singing over these words of Scripture to myself; and went to prayer, to pray to God that I might enjoy Him; and prayed in a manner quite different from what I used to do; with a new sort of affection. But it never came into my thought, that there was anything spiritual, or of a saving nature in this.

From about that time, I began to have a new kind of apprehensions and ideas of Christ, and the work of redemption, and the glorious way of salvation by Him. I had an inward, sweet sense of these things, that at times came into my heart; and my soul was led away in pleasant views and contemplations of them. And my mind was greatly engaged, to spend my time in reading and meditating on Christ; and the beauty and excellency of His person, and the lovely way of salvation, by free grace in Him. I found no books so delightful to me, as those that treated of these subjects....

Not long after I first began to experience these things, I gave an account to my father, of some things that had passed in my mind. I was pretty much affected by the discourse we had together. And when the discourse was ended, I walked abroad alone, in a solitary place in my father's pasture, for contemplation. And as I was walking there, and looked up on the sky and clouds, there came into my mind a sweet sense of the glorious majesty and grace of God, that I know not how to express. I seemed to see them both in a sweet conjunction: majesty and meekness joined together: it was a sweet and gentle, and holy majesty; and also a majestic meekness; an awful sweetness; a high, and great, and holy gentleness.

After this my sense of divine things gradually increased, and became more and more lively, and had more of that inward sweetness. The appearance of everything was altered; there seemed to be, as it were, a calm, sweet cast, or appearance of divine glory, in almost everything. God's excellency, His wisdom, His purity and love, seemed to appear in everything; in the sun, moon and stars; in the clouds, and blue sky; in the grass, flowers, trees; in the water, and all nature; which used greatly to fix my mind. I often used to sit and view the moon, for a long time; and so in the daytime, spent much time in viewing the clouds and sky, to behold the sweet glory of God in these things: in the meantime, singing forth with a low voice, my contemplations of the Creator and Redeemer. And scarce anything, among all the works of nature, was so sweet to me as thunder and lightning. Formerly, nothing had been so terrible to me. I used to be a person uncommonly terrified with thunder; and it used to strike me with terror, when I saw a thunderstorm rising. But now, on the contrary, it rejoiced me. I felt God at the first appearance of a thunderstorm. And used to take the opportunity at such times to fix myself to view the clouds, and see the lightnings play, and hear the majestic and awful voice of God's thunder: which oftentimes was exceeding entertaining, leading me to sweet contemplations of my great and glorious God. And while I viewed, used to spend my time, as it always seemed natural to me, to sing or chant forth my meditations; to speak my thoughts in soliloquies, and speak with a singing voice.

I felt then a great satisfaction as to my good estate. But that did not content me. I had vehement longings of soul after God and Christ, and after more holiness; wherewith my heart seemed to be full, and ready to break: which often brought to my mind, the words of the psalmist: *"My soul breaketh for the longing it hath"* (Psalm 119:20). I often felt a mourning and lamenting in my heart, that I had not turned to God sooner, that I might have had more time to grow in grace. My mind was greatly fixed on divine things; I was almost perpetually in the contemplation of them. Spent most of my time in thinking of divine things, year after year. And used to spend abundance of my time, in walking alone in the woods, and solitary places, for meditation, soliloquy and prayer, and converse with God. And it was always my manner, at such times, to sing forth my contemplations. And was almost constantly in ejaculatory prayer, wherever I was. Prayer seemed to be natural to me; as the breath, by which the inward burnings of my heart had vent....

My sense of divine things seemed gradually to increase, till I went to preach at New York; which was about a year and a half after they began. While I was there, I felt them, very sensibly, in a much higher degree, than I had done before. My longings after God and holiness, were much increased. Pure and humble, holy and heavenly Christianity, appeared exceeding amiable to me. I felt in me a burning desire to be in everything a complete Christian; and conformed to the blessed image of Christ: and that I might live in all things, according to the pure, sweet and blessed rules of the gospel. I had an eager thirsting after progress in these things. My longings after it, put me upon pursuing and pressing after them. It was my continual strife day and night, and constant inquiry, how I should be more holy, and live more holily, and more becoming a child of God, and disciple of Christ. I sought an increase of grace and holiness, and that I might live an holy life, with vastly more earnestness, than ever I sought grace, before I had it. I used to be continually examining myself, and studying and contriving for likely ways and means, how I should live holily, with far greater diligence and earnestness, than ever I pursued anything in my life. But with too great a dependence on my own strength; which afterwards proved a great damage to me. My experience had not then taught me, as it has done since, my extreme feebleness and impotence, every manner of way; and the innumerable and bottomless depths of secret corruption and deceit, that there was in my heart. However, I went on with my eager pursuit after more holiness; and sweet conformity to Christ.

The heaven I desired was a heaven of holiness; to be with God, and to spend my eternity in divine love, and holy communion with Christ. My mind was very much taken up with contemplations on heaven, and the enjoyments of those there; and living there in perfect holiness, humility and love. And it used at that time to appear a great part of the happiness of heaven, that there the saints could express their love to Christ. It appeared to me a great clog and hindrance and burden to me, that what I felt within, I could not express to God, and give vent to, as I desired. The inward ardor of my soul, seemed to be hindered and pent up, and could not freely flame out as it would. I used often to think, how in heaven, this sweet principle should freely and fully vent and express itself. Heaven appeared to me exceeding delightful as a world of love. It appeared to me, that all happiness consisted in living in pure, humble, heavenly, divine love.

I remember the thoughts I used then to have of holiness. I remember I then said sometimes to myself, I do certainly know that I love holiness, such as the gospel prescribes. It appeared to me, there was nothing in it but what was ravishingly lovely. It appeared to me, to be the highest beauty and amiableness, above all other beauties: that it was a *divine* beauty; far purer than anything here upon earth; and that everything else, was like mire, filth and defilement, in comparison of it.

Holiness, as I then wrote down some of my

contemplations on it, appeared to me to be of a sweet, pleasant, charming, serene, calm nature. It seemed to me, it brought an inexpressible purity, brightness, peacefulness and ravishment to the soul: and that it made the soul like a field or garden of God, with all manner of pleasant flowers; that is all pleasant, delightful and undisturbed; enjoying a sweet calm, and the gently vivifying beams of the sun. The soul of a true Christian, as I then wrote my meditations, appeared like such a little white flower, as we see in the spring of the year; low and humble on the ground, opening its bosom, to receive the pleasant beams of the sun's glory; rejoicing as it were, in a calm rapture; diffusing around a sweet fragrancy; standing peacefully and lovingly, in the midst of other flowers round about; all in like manner opening their bosoms, to drink in the light of the sun....

It has often appeared sweet to me, to be united to Christ; to have Him for my Head, and to be a member of His body: and also to have Christ for my Teacher and Prophet. I very often think with sweetness and longings and pantings of soul, of being a little child, taking hold of Christ, to be led by Him through the wilderness of this world. That text, Matthew 18, near at the beginning, has often been sweet to me, *"Except ye be converted, and become as little children...."* I love to think of coming to Christ, to receive salvation of Him, poor in spirit, and quite empty of self; humbly exalting Him alone; cut entirely off from my own root, and to grow into, and out of Christ: to have God in Christ to be all in all; and to live by faith on the Son of God, a life of humble, unfeigned confidence in Him. That Scripture has often been sweet to me. *"Not unto us, O Lord, not unto us, but unto thy name give glory, for thy mercy, and for thy truth's sake"* (Psalm 115:1). And those words of Christ: *"In that hour Jesus rejoiced in spirit, and said, I thank thee, O Father, Lord of heaven and earth, that thou hast hid these things from the wise and prudent, and hast revealed them unto babes: even so, Father; for so it seemed good in thy sight"* (Luke 10:21). That sovereignty of God that Christ rejoiced in, seemed to me to be worthy to be rejoiced in; and that rejoicing of Christ, seemed to me to show the excellency of Christ, and the Spirit that He was of....

The sweetest joys and delights I have experienced have not been those that have arisen from a hope of my own good estate; but in a direct view of the glorious things of the gospel. When I enjoy this sweetness, it seems to carry me above the thoughts of my own safe estate. It seems at such times a loss that I cannot bear, to take off my eye from the glorious, pleasant object I behold without me, to turn my eye in upon myself, and my own good estate....

2

Personal Resolutions

The description of his experience, like that of many others, expresses a rapturous desire to sit with Christ in heavenly places. But it would be wrong to conclude that it was only an ecstatic feeling. There was a methodical discipline of will which undergirded his devotion and directed his life. This comes through clearly in his *Resolutions.*

These seventy intentions were drawn up during his graduate study and before his settlement at Northampton. It was not unusual for sensitive young people of that day to define for themselves goals of life, and to set standards of conduct by which their aspirations might be realized. Because these resolves express so earnestly a heart panting after God, they are cited here in full.

Being sensible that I am unable to do anything without God's help, I do humbly entreat Him by His grace, to enable me to keep these Resolutions, so far as they are agreeable to His will, for Christ's sake.

Remember to Read over These Resolutions Once a Week

1. *Resolved,* That *I will do whatsoever* I think to be most to the glory of God and my own good, profit and pleasure, in the whole of my duration; without any consideration of the time, whether now, or never so many myriads of ages hence. Resolved to do whatever I think to be my *duty,* and most for the good and advantage of mankind in general. Resolved, so to do, whatever *difficulties* I meet with, how many soever, and how great soever.

2. *Resolved,* To be continually endeavoring to find out some *new contrivance,* and invention, to promote the forementioned things.

3. *Resolved,* If ever I shall fall and grow dull, so as to neglect to keep any part of these Resolutions, to repent of all I can remember, when I come to myself again.

4. *Resolved,* Never *to do* any manner of thing, whether in soul or body, less or more, but what tends to the glory of God, nor *be,* nor *suffer* it, if I can possibly avoid it.

5. *Resolved,* Never to lose one moment of time, but to improve it in the most profitable way I possibly can.

6. *Resolved,* To live with all my might, while I do live.

7. *Resolved,* Never to do anything, which I should be afraid to do, if it were the last hour of my life.

8. *Resolved,* To act, in all respects, both

speaking and doing, as if nobody had been so vile as I, and as if I had committed the same sins, or had the same infirmities or failings as others; and that I will let the knowledge of their failings promote nothing but shame in myself, and prove only an occasion of my confessing my own sins and misery to God. *Vid. July 30.*

9. *Resolved,* To think much, on all occasions, of my own dying, and of the common circumstances which attend death.

10. *Resolved,* When I feel pain, to think of the pains of martyrdom, and of hell.

11. Resolved, When I think of any theorem in divinity to be solved, immediately to do what I can towards solving it, if circumstances do not hinder.

12. *Resolved,* If I take delight in it as a gratification of pride, or vanity, or on any such account, immediately to throw it by.

13. *Resolved,* To be endeavoring to find out fit objects of charity and liberality.

14. *Resolved,* Never to do anything out of revenge.

15. *Resolved,* Never to suffer the least motions of anger towards irrational beings.

16. *Resolved,* Never to speak evil of anyone, so that it shall tend to his dishonor, more or less, upon no account except for some real good.

17. *Resolved,* That I will live so, as I shall wish I had done when I come to die.

18. *Resolved,* To live so, at all times, as I think is best in my most devout frames, and

when I have the clearest notions of the things of the gospel, and another world.

19. *Resolved,* Never to do anything, which I should be afraid to do, if I expected it would not be above an hour, before I should hear the last trumpet.

20. *Resolved,* To maintain the strictest temperance, in eating and drinking.

21. *Resolved,* Never to do anything, which if I should see in another, I should count a just occasion to despise him for, or to think any way the more meanly of him.

22. *Resolved,* To endeavor to obtain for myself as much happiness, in the other world, as I possibly can, with all the power, might, vigor, and vehemence, yea violence, I am capable of, or can bring myself to exert, in any way that can be thought of.

23. *Resolved,* Frequently to take some deliberate action, which seems most unlikely to be done, for the glory of God, and trace it back to the original intention, designs and ends of it; and if I find it not to be for God's glory, to repute it as a breach of the fourth Resolution.

24. *Resolved,* Whenever I do any conspicuously evil action, to trace it back, till I come to the original cause; and then, both carefully endeavor to do so no more, and to fight and pray with all my might against the original of it.

25. *Resolved,* To examine carefully, and constantly, what that one thing in me is, which causes me in the least to doubt of the love of God; and to direct all my forces against it.

26. *Resolved,* To cast away such things, as I find do abate my assurance.

27. *Resolved,* Never willfully to omit anything, except the omission be for glory of God; and frequently to examine my omissions.

28. *Resolved,* To study the Scriptures so steadily, constantly and frequently, so that I may find, and plainly perceive myself to grow in the knowledge of the same.

29. *Resolved,* Never to count that a prayer, nor to let that pass as a prayer, nor that as a petition of a prayer, which is so made, that I cannot hope that God will answer it; nor that as a confession, which I cannot hope God will accept.

30. *Resolved,* To strive, every week, to be brought higher in religion, and to a higher exercise of grace, than I was the week before.

31. *Resolved,* Never to say anything at all against anybody, but when it is perfectly agreeable to the highest degree of Christian honor, and of love to mankind, agreeable to the lowest humility, and sense of my own faults and failings, and agreeable to the Golden Rule; often, when I have said anything against anyone, to bring it to, and try it strictly by the test of this Resolution.

32. *Resolved,* To be strictly and firmly faithful to my trust, that that, in Proverbs 20:6, *"A faithful man, who can find?"* may not be partly fulfilled in me.

33. *Resolved,* To do, always, what I can towards making, maintaining and preserving peace, when it can be done without an overbalancing

detriment in other respects. *Dec. 26, 1722.*

34. *Resolved,* In narrations, never to speak anything but the pure and simple verity.

35. *Resolved,* Whenever I so much question whether I have done my duty, as that my quiet and calm is thereby disturbed, to set it down, and also how the question was resolved. *Dec. 18, 1722.*

36. *Resolved,* Never to speak evil of any, except I have some particular good call to it. *Dec. 19, 1722.*

37. *Resolved,* To inquire every night, as I am going to bed: Wherein I have been negligent? What sin I have committed? and Wherein I have denied myself? also, at the end of every week, month, and year. *Dec. 22 and 26, 1722.*

38. *Resolved,* Never to utter anything that is sportive, or matter of laughter, on a Lord's day. *Sabbath evening, Dec. 23, 1722.*

39. *Resolved,* Never to do anything, of which I so much question the lawfulness, as that I intend, at the same time, to consider and examine afterwards, whether it be lawful or not; unless I as much question the lawfulness of the omission.

40. *Resolved,* To inquire every night, before I go to bed, whether I have acted in the best way I possibly could, with respect to eating and drinking. *Jan. 7, 1723.*

41. *Resolved,* To ask myself, at the end of every day, week, month, and year, wherein I could possibly, in any respect, have done better. *Jan. 11, 1723.*

42. *Resolved,* Frequently to renew the dedication of myself to God, which was made at my baptism, which I solemnly renewed, when I was received into the communion of the church, and which I have solemnly remade this 12th day of January, 1723.

43. *Resolved,* Never, henceforward, till I die, to act as if I were any way my own, but entirely and altogether God's; agreeably to what is to be found in Saturday, January 12th. *Jan. 12th, 1723.*

44. *Resolved,* That no other end but religion, shall have any influence at all on any of my actions; and that no action shall be, in the least circumstance, any otherwise than the religious end will carry it. *Jan. 12, 1723.*

45. *Resolved,* Never to allow any pleasure or grief, joy or sorrow, nor any affection at all, nor any degree of affection, nor any circumstance relating to it, but what helps Religion. *Jan. 12 and 13, 1723.*

46. *Resolved,* Never to allow the least measure of any fretting or uneasiness at my father or mother. *Resolved,* To suffer no effects of it, so much as in the least alteration of speech, or motion of my eye; and to be especially careful of it with respect to any of our family.

47. *Resolved,* To endeavor, to my utmost, to deny whatever is not most agreeable to a good and universally sweet and benevolent quiet, peaceable, contented and easy, compassionate and generous, humble and meek, submissive and obliging, diligent and industrious, charitable and even, patient, moderate, forgiving and

sincere, temper; and to do, at all times, what such a temper would lead me to; and to examine strictly, at the end of every week, whether I have so done. *Sabbath morning, May 5, 1723.*

48. *Resolved,* Constantly, with the utmost niceness and diligence, and the strictest scrutiny, to be looking into the state of my soul, that I may know whether I have truly an interest in Christ or not; that when I come to die, I may not have any negligence respecting this, to repent of. *May 26, 1723.*

49. *Resolved,* That this never shall be, if I can help it.

50. *Resolved,* That I will act so, as I think I shall judge would have been best, and most prudent, when I come into the future world. *July 5, 1723.*

51. *Resolved,* That I will act so, in every respect, as I think I shall wish I had done, if I should at last be damned. *July 8, 1723.*

52. I frequently hear persons in old age, say how they would live, if they were to live their lives over again: *Resolved,* That I will live just so as I can think I shall wish I had done, supposing I live to old age. *July 8, 1723.*

53. *Resolved,* To improve every opportunity, when I am in the best and happiest frame of mind, to cast and venture my soul on the Lord Jesus Christ, to trust and confide in Him, and consecrate myself wholly to Him; that from this I may have assurance of my safety, knowing that I confide in my Redeemer. *July 8, 1723.*

54. *Resolved,* Whenever I hear anything spo-

ken in commendation of any person, if I think it would be praiseworthy in me, that I will endeavor to imitate it. *July 8, 1723.*

55. *Resolved,* To endeavor, to my utmost, so to act, as I can think I should do, if I had already seen the happiness of heaven, and hell torments. *July 8, 1723.*

56. *Resolved,* Never to give over, nor in the least to slacken, my fight with my corruptions, however unsuccessful I may be.

57. *Resolved,* When I fear misfortunes and adversity, to examine whether I have done my duty, and resolve to do it, and let the event be just as Providence orders it. I will, as far as I can, be concerned about nothing but my duty, and my sin. *June 9 and July 13, 1723.*

58. *Resolved,* Not only to refrain from an air of dislike, fretfulness and anger in conversation, but to exhibit an air of love, cheerfulness and benignity. *May 27 and July 13, 1723.*

59. *Resolved,* When I am most conscious of provocations to ill nature and anger, that I will strive most to feel and act good-naturedly; yea, at such times, to manifest good nature, though I think that in other respects it would be disadvantageous, and so as would be imprudent at other times. *May 12, July 11, and July 13.*

60. *Resolved,* Whenever my feelings begin to appear in the least out of order, when I am conscious of the least uneasiness within, or the least irregularity without, I will then subject myself to the strictest examination. *July 4 and 13, 1723.*

61. *Resolved,* That I will not give way to that listlessness which I find unbends and relaxes my mind from being fully and fixedly set on religion, whatever excuse I may have for it—that what my listlessness inclines me to do, is best to be done, etc. *May 21 and July 13, 1723.*

62. *Resolved,* Never to do anything but my duty, and then according to Ephesians 6:6–8, to do it willingly and cheerfully, as unto the Lord, and not to man: knowing that whatever good thing any man doth, the same shall he receive of the Lord. *June 25 and July 13, 1723.*

63. On the supposition, that there never was to be but one individual in the world, at any one time, who was properly a complete Christian, in all respects of a right stamp, having Christianity always shining in its true lustre, and appearing excellent and lovely, from whatever part and under whatever character viewed: *Resolved,* To act just as I would do, if I strove with all my might to be that one, who should live in my time. *Jan. 14 and July 13, 1723.*

64. *Resolved,* When I find those *"groanings which cannot be uttered,"* of which the apostle speaks, and those *"breakings of soul* for the longing it hath,"* of which the psalmist speaks (Psalm 119), that I will promote them to the utmost of my power, and that I will not be weary of earnestly endeavoring to vent my desires, nor of the repetitions of such earnestness. *July 23 and Aug. 10, 1723.*

65. *Resolved,* very much to exercise myself in this, all my life long, *viz.,* with the greatest

openness, of which I am capable, to declare my ways to God, and lay open my soul to Him, all my sins, temptations, difficulties, sorrows, fears, hopes, desires, and everything, and every circumstance, according to Dr. Manton's sermon on Psalm 119. *July 26 and Aug. 10, 1723.*

66. *Resolved,* That I will endeavor always to keep a benign aspect, and air of acting and speaking in all places, and in all companies, except it should so happen that duty requires otherwise.

67. *Resolved,* After afflictions, to inquire, What I am the better for them? What good I have got by them? and What I might have got by them?

68. *Resolved,* To confess frankly to myself all that which I find in myself, either infirmity or sin; and, if it be what concerns religion, also to confess the whole case to God, and implore needed help. *July 23 and Aug. 10, 1723.*

69. *Resolved,* Always to do that, which I shall wish I had done when I see others do it. *Aug. 11, 1723.*

70. Let there be something of benevolence, in all that I speak. *Aug. 17, 1723.*

3

Constant Review

———

The fidelity with which Edwards sought to keep these commitments may be seen in his *Diary.* He began to make these notations about the same time as his *Resolutions,* and continued with interruptions until 1735. A check upon his accomplishments in fulfilling the resolves, the journal shows a conscious quest in spiritual self-discipline. There is no attempt to build up himself in his own eyes. Rather he tells it like it is —his joy and his despair, his success and his failure. Here is revealed a man's burning desire to bring his soul under the refining light of God's holiness. The following excerpts are representative:

December, 1722

Dec. 18. This day made the 35th Resolution. The reason why I, in the least, question my interest in God's love and favor, is 1. Because I cannot speak so fully to my experience of that preparatory work, of which divines speak. 2. I do not remember that I experienced regeneration, exactly in those steps, in which divines say it is generally wrought. 3. I do not feel the Christian graces sensibly enough, particularly faith. I fear they are only such hypocritical outside affections, which wicked men may feel, as well as others. They do not seem to be sufficiently inward, full, sincere, entire and hearty. They do not seem so substantial, and so wrought into my very nature, as I could wish. 4. Because I am sometimes guilty of sins of omission and commission. Lately I have doubted, whether I do not transgress in evil speaking. This day, resolved.

Dec. 21, Friday. This day, and yesterday, I was exceedingly, dull, dry and dead.

Dec. 22, Saturday. This day, revived by God's Holy Spirit; affected with the sense of the excellency of holiness, felt more exercise of love to Christ, than usual. Have, also, felt sensible repentance for sin, because it was committed against so merciful and good a God. This night made the 37th Resolution.

Monday, Dec. 24. Higher thoughts than usual of the excellency of Christ and His kingdom. Concluded to observe, at the end of every month, the number of breaches of Resolutions, to see whether they increase or diminish, to begin from this day, and to compute from that weekly account, my monthly increase and, out of the whole, my yearly increase, beginning from new year days.

1722-23. Tuesday, Jan. 1. Have been dull for several days. Examined whether I have not been guilty of negligence today; and resolved.

Wednesday, Jan. 2. Dull. I find, by experience, that, let me make Resolutions, and do what I will, with never so many inventions, it is all nothing, and to no purpose at all, without the motions of the Spirit of God; for if the Spirit of God should be as much withdrawn from me always, as for the week past, notwithstanding all I do, I should not grow, but should languish, and miserably fade away. I perceive, if God should withdraw His Spirit a little more, I should not hesitate to break my Resolutions, and should soon arrive at my old state. There is no dependence on myself. Our resolutions may be the highest one day, and yet, the next day, we may be in a miserable dead condition, not at all like the same person who resolved. So that it is to no purpose to resolve, except we depend on the grace of God. For, if it were not for His mere grace, one might be a very good man one day, and a very wicked one the next. I find also by experience, that there is no guessing on the ends of Providence, in particular dispensations towards me—any otherwise than as afflictions come as corrections for sin, and God intends when we meet with them, to desire us to look back on our ways, and see wherein we have done amiss, and lament that particular sin, and all our sins, before Him—knowing this, also, that all things shall work together for our good; not knowing in what way, indeed, but trusting in God.

Sabbath, Jan. 6. At night. Much concerned about the improvement of precious time. Intend to live in continual mortification, without ceasing, and even to weary myself thereby, as long as I am in this world, and never to expect or desire any worldly ease or pleasure.

Saturday, Jan. 12. In the morning. I have this day, solemnly renewed my baptismal covenant and self-dedication, which I renewed, when I was taken into the communion of the church. I have been before God, and have given myself, all that I am, and have, to God; so that I am not, in any respect, my own. I can challenge no right in this understanding, this will, these affections, which are in me. Neither have I any right to this body, or any of its members—no right to this tongue, these hands, these feet; no right to these senses, these eyes, these ears, this smell, or this taste. I have given myself clear away, and have not retained anything, as my own. I gave myself to God, in my baptism, and I have been this morning to Him, and told Him, that I gave myself *wholly* to Him. I have given every power to Him; so that for the future, I'll challenge no right in myself, in no respect whatever, I have expressly promised Him, and I do now promise Almighty God, that by His grace, I will not. I have this morning told Him that I did take Him for my whole portion and felicity, looking on nothing else, as any part of my happiness, nor acting as if it were; and His law, for the constant rule of my obedience; and would fight, with all my might, against the world, the flesh and the devil, to the end of my life; and that I did believe in Jesus Christ, and did receive Him as a Prince and Savior; and that I would adhere to the faith and obedience of the gospel, however hazardous and difficult, the confession and practice of it may be; and that I did receive the blessed Spirit, as my Teacher, Sanctifier, and only Comforter, and cherish all His motions to enlighten, purify, confirm, comfort and assist me. This, I have done; and I pray God, for the sake of Christ, to look upon it as a self-dedication, and to receive me now, as entirely His own, and to deal with me, in all respects, as such, whether He afflicts me, or prospers me, or whatever He pleases to do with me, who am His. Now, henceforth, I am not to act, in any respect, as my own. I shall act as my own, if I ever make use of any of my powers, to anything, that is not to the glory of God, and do not make the glorifying of Him, my whole and entire business—if I murmur in the least at affliction; if I grieve at the prosperity of others; if I am in any way uncharitable; if I am angry, because of injuries; if I revenge them; if I do anything, purely to please myself, or if I avoid anything, for the sake of my own ease; if I omit anything, because it is great self-denial; if I trust to myself; if I take any of the praise of any good that I do, or that God doth by me; or if I am in any way proud. This day, made the 42d and 43d Resolutions.

Saturday, Feb. 16. I do certainly know that I love holiness, such as the gospel prescribes. *At night.* For the time past of my life, I have been negligent, in that I have not sufficiently kept up that part of divine worship, singing the praise of God in secret, and with company. I have been negligent the month past, in these three things. I have not been watchful enough over my appetites, in eating and drinking; in rising too late in the morning; and in not applying myself with sufficient application to the duty of secret prayer.

Sabbath day, Feb. 17. Near sunset. Renewedly promised, that I will accept of God for my whole portion, and that I will be contented, whatever else I am denied. I will not murmur nor be grieved, whatever prosperity upon any account I see others enjoy, and I am denied. To this I have lately acted contrary.

Monday morning, April 1. I think it best not to allow myself to laugh at the faults, follies and infirmities, of others.

Wednesday forenoon, May 1. I have always, in every different state of life I have hitherto been in, thought that the troubles and difficulties of that state were greater, than those of any other state that I proposed to be in; and when I have altered, with assurance of mending myself, I have still thought the same, yea that the difficulties of that state are greater than those of that I left last. Lord, grant that from hence I may learn to withdraw my thoughts, affections, desires and expectations entirely from the world, and may fix them upon the heavenly state, where there is fullness of joy; where reigns heavenly, sweet, calm and delightful love without alloy; where there are continually the dearest expressions of this love: where there is the enjoyment of this love without ever parting; and where those persons, who appear so lovely in this world, will be inexpressibly more lovely, and full of love to us. How sweetly will those, who thus mutually love, join together in singing the praises of God and the Lamb. How full will it fill us with joy, to think that this enjoyment, these sweet exercises, will never cease or come to an end, but will last to all eternity.

Saturday night, May 4. Although I have, in some measure, subdued a disposition to chide and fret, yet I find a certain inclination, which is not agreeable to Christian sweetness of temper and conversation: either too much dogmaticalness or too much egotism, a disposition to manifest my own dislike and scorn, and my own freedom from those which are innocent, sinless, yea common infirmities of men, and many other such like things. O that God would help me to discover all the flaws and defects of my temper and conversation, and help me in the difficult work of amending them; and that He would grant me so full a measure of vital Christianity, that the foundation of all these disagreeable irregularities may be destroyed, and the contrary sweetnesses and beauties may of themselves naturally follow.

Tuesday afternoon, July 23. When I find those *groanings which cannot be uttered,* of which the apostle speaks, and those *soul-breakings for the longing it hath,* of which the psalmist speaks (Psalm 119:20), *Resolved,* to favor and promote them to the utmost of my power, and not to be weary of earnestly endeavoring to vent my desires, and not to be weary of the repetitions of such earnestness.

To count it all joy, when I have occasions of great self-denial; because, then, I have a glorious opportunity of giving deadly wounds to the body of sin, and of greatly confirming, and establishing the new creature. I seek to mortify sin, and increase in holiness.

Tuesday night, July 30. Have concluded to endeavor to work myself into duties by searching and tracing back all the real reasons why I do them not, and narrowly searching out all the subtle subterfuge of my thoughts, and answering them to the utmost of my power, that I may know what are the very first originals of my defect, as with respect to want of repentance, love to God, loathing of myself—to do this sometimes in sermons. *Vid. Resolution 8.* Especially, to take occasion therefrom, to bewail those sins of which I have been guilty, that are akin to them; as for instance, from pride in others, to take occasion to bewail my pride; from their malice, to take occasion to bewail the same in myself: when I am evil-spoken of, to take occasion to bewail my evil speaking: and so of other sins. *Mem.* To receive slanders and reproaches, as glorious opportunities of doing this.

Friday afternoon, Aug. 9. With respect to the important business which I have now on hand.

Resolved, To do whatever I think to be duty, prudence and diligence in the matter, and to avoid ostentation; and if I succeed not, and how many disappointments soever I meet with, to be entirely easy; only to take occasion to acknowledge my unworthiness; and if it should actually not succeed, and should not find acceptance, as I expected, yet not to afflict myself about it, according to the 57th Resolution. *At night.* One thing that may be a good help towards thinking profitably in times of vacation, is, when I find a profitable thought that I can fix my mind on, to follow it as far as I possibly can to advantage.—I missed it, when a graduate at college, both in point of duty and prudence, in going against a universal benevolence and good nature.

Saturday morning, Aug. 24. Have not practiced quite right about revenge; though I have not done anything directly out of revenge, yet, I have perhaps, omitted some things, that I should otherwise have done, or have altered the circumstances and manner of my actions, hoping for a secret sort of revenge thereby. I have felt a little sort of satisfaction, when I thought that such an evil would happen to them by my actions, as would make them repent what they have done. To be satisfied for their repenting, when they repent from a sense of their error, is right. But a satisfaction in their repentance, because of the evil that is brought upon them, is revenge. This is in some measure, a taking the matter out of God's hands when He was about to manage it, who is better able to plead it for me. Well, therefore, may He leave me to boggle at it.

Wednesday night, Aug. 28. When I want books to read; yea, when I have not very good books, not to spend time in reading them, but in reading the Scriptures, in perusing Resolutions, Reflections, etc., in writing on Types of the Scripture, and other things, in studying the languages, and in spending more time in private duties. To do this, when there is a prospect of wanting time for the purpose. Remember as soon as I can, to get a piece of *slate,* or something, whereon I can make short memorandums while traveling.

Thursday, Aug. 29. Two great *Quaerenda* with me now are: How shall I take advantage of all the time I spend in journeys? And how shall I make a glorious improvement of afflictions?

Monday, Sept. 23. I observe that old men seldom have any advantage of new discoveries, because they are beside the way of thinking, to which they have been so long used. *Resolved,* if ever I live to years, that I will be impartial to hear the reasons of all pretended discoveries, and receive them if rational, how long soever I have been used to another way of thinking. My time is so short, that I have not time to perfect myself in all studies: Wherefore resolved, to omit and put off, all but the most important and needful studies.

Tuesday forenoon, Nov. 26. It is a most evil and pernicious practice, in meditations on afflictions, to sit ruminating on the aggravations of the affliction, and reckoning up the evil, dark circumstances thereof, and dwelling long on the dark side: it doubles and trebles the affliction. And so, when speaking of them to others, to make them as bad as we can, and use our eloquence to set forth our own troubles, is to be all the while making new trouble, and feeding and pampering the old; whereas, the contrary practice, would starve our affliction. If we dwelt on the bright side of things in our thoughts, and extenuated them all that we possibly could, when speaking of them, we should think little of them ourselves, and the affliction would, really, in a great measure, vanish away.

Friday morning, Dec. 27. At the end of every month, to examine my behavior strictly, by some chapter in the New Testament, more especially made up of rules of life. At the end of the year, to examine my behavior by the rules of the New Testament in general, reading many chapters. It would also be convenient, some time at the end of the year, to read, for this purpose, in the Book of Proverbs.

Saturday, Feb. 22. I observe that there are some evil habits, which do increase and grow stronger, even in some good people, as they grow older; habits that much obscure the beauty of Christianity: some things which are according to their natural tempers, which, in some measure, prevails when they are young in Christ, and the evil disposition, having an unobserved control, the habit at last grows very strong, and commonly regulates the practice until death. By this means, old Christians are very commonly, in some respects, more unreasonable than those who are young. I am afraid of contracting such habits, particularly of grudging to give, and to do, and of procrastinating.

Sabbath, Feb. 23. I must be contented, where I have anything strange or remarkable to tell, not to make it appear so remarkable as it is indeed; lest through the fear of this, and the desire of making a thing appear very remarkable, I should exceed the bounds of simple verity.

Sabbath, Nov. 22. Considering that bystanders always copy some faults, which we do not see, ourselves, or of which, at least, we are not so fully sensible; and that there are many secret workings of corruption, which escape our sight, and of which, others only are sensible: *Resolved,* therefore, that I will, if I can by any convenient means, learn what faults others find in me, or what things they see in me, that appear any way blameworthy, unlovely, or unbecoming.

April 4, 1735. When at any time, I have a sense of any divine thing, then to turn it in my thoughts, to a practical improvement. As for instance, when I am in my mind on some argument for the truth of religion, the reality of a future state, and the like, then to think with myself, how safely I may venture to sell all, for a future good. So when, at any time, I have a more than ordinary sense of the glory of the saints, in another world; to think how well it is worth my while, to deny myself, and to sell all that I have for this glory, etc.

————

So beat the heart of Jonathan Edwards, truly an extraordinary man by any measure. His penetrating insights into the reality of things have justly earned him a place in America's Hall of Fame. But however one may view his legacy, he must be regarded as a saintly scholar. It was his simple faith and childlike piety which gave distinction to his other gifts. He could not tolerate the sham of human self-sufficiency, most of all when it masqueraded under the guise of intelligence. To him the fear of God was the beginning of wisdom. Yet it was a holy fear founded upon an implicit trust in the grace of a loving Savior. Jesus commanded his obedience. As few men of his age, he resolved to dedicate all his mind, all his soul, all his strength to the praise of his majestic Lord.

Should we not make the same resolution?

Notes

Notes

Notes

Notes

Notes

Notes

Notes

Notes

Notes

Notes

Notes

Notes

Notes

Notes

Notes

Notes

Notes